THE WHITE HOUSE

by Brittany Cesky

WEST HARTFORD

Baby Koala
An Imprint of Pop!
popbooksonline.com

9160

PUBLIC LIBRARY

abdopublishing.com
Published by Pop!, a division of ABDO, PO Box 398166, Minneapolis, Minnesota 55439. Copyright © 2019 by POP, LLC. International copyrights reserved in all countries. No part of this book may be reproduced in any form without written permission from the publisher. Pop!™ is a trademark and logo of POP, LLC.

Printed in the United States of America, North Mankato, Minnesota.

042018
092018

 THIS BOOK CONTAINS RECYCLED MATERIALS

Distributed in paperback by North Star Editions, Inc.

Cover Photo: iStockphoto
Interior Photos: iStockphoto, 5, 6, 14, 16–17, 20; Haraz N. Ghanbari/AP Images, 9; Carolyn Kaster/AP Images, 10; Bettmann/Getty Images, 13; Shutterstock Images, 19 (top), 19 (bottom left), 19 (bottom right)

Editor: Meg Gaertner
Series Designer: Laura Mitchell

Library of Congress Control Number: 2017963466
Publisher's Cataloging-in-Publication Data
Names: Cesky, Brittany, author.
Title: The White House / by Brittany Cesky.
Description: Minneapolis, Minnesota : Pop!, 2019. | Series: US symbols | Includes online resources and index.
Identifiers: ISBN 9781532160509 (lib.bdg.) | ISBN 9781635178388 (pbk) | ISBN 9781532161629 (ebook) |
Subjects: LCSH: White House (Washington, D.C.)--Juvenile literature. | Washington (D.C.)--Buildings, structures, etc--Juvenile literature. | Signs and symbols--United States--Juvenile literature. | Emblems, National--Juvenile literature.
Classification: DDC 975.3--dc23

Hello! My name is

Cody Koala

Pop open this book and you'll find QR codes like this one, loaded with information, so you can learn even more!

Scan this code* and others like it while you read, or visit the website below to make this book pop.

popbooksonline.com/the-white-house

*requires a web-enabled smart device with a QR code reader app and a camera.

PJJ
YELLOW

Table of Contents

Chapter 1

Leadership

The US President lives in the White House. It is a **symbol** of the US government. It also stands for freedom.

Watch a video here!

White House

The White House is in Washington, DC. That city is America's **capital**. The government meets and works there.

People can visit the White House and take a free **tour**.

Chapter 2

History

Presidents have lived in the White House for hundreds of years. They can make changes to the White House. They might buy new rugs or tables.

Complete an activity here!

Oval Office, in the West Wing

Over time, presidents added **wings** to make the building bigger. There are hundreds of rooms in the White House today. They are spread out over six floors.

The first president to live in the White House was John Adams in 1800.

Chapter 3

Inside the White House

The president's family lives in the middle part of the White House. There are also meeting rooms in this part of the house.

Learn more here!

Reporters go to the west **terrace** to hear news from the president.

The White House also has a pool and places to play basketball, tennis, golf, and bowling.

The president's office is
in the West Wing. There are
also rooms for reporters.

The East Wing is home to more offices. The east terrace has a movie theater.

Chapter 4

Importance

Presidents hold important events at the White House to honor great Americans. Presidents also welcome world leaders to visit the White House.

Learn more here!

These visits help build

peace. They build good

relationships between the

United States and other countries. The White House is a symbol of US leadership in the world.

Making Connections

Text-to-Self

How is the White House different from your home? How is it similar?

Text-to-Text

Have you read other books about the White House? What new information did you learn from reading this book?

Text-to-World

The White House is often in the news. What stories have you heard about it lately?

Glossary

capital – the city in which a government meets and works.

relationship – the way in which people get along.

symbol – something that stands for something else because of certain similarities.

terrace – a walkway connecting two parts of a building.

tour – a guided trip along a set path.

wing – part of a building that spreads out from the main part.

Index

Online Resources

popbooksonline.com

Thanks for reading this Cody Koala book!

Scan this code* and others like it in this book, or visit the website below to make this book pop!

popbooksonline.com/the-white-house

*Scanning QR codes requires a web-enabled smart device with a QR code reader app and a camera.